MAKER MODELS

FAIRGROUND

Anna Claybourne

First published in Great Britain in 2019
by Wayland
Copyright © Hodder & Stoughton
All rights reserved

Editor: Elise Short
Design and illustration: Collaborate

HB ISBN: 978 1 5263 0743 9
PB ISBN: 978 1 5263 0744 6

Printed and bound in China

Wayland, an imprint of
Hachette Children's Group
Part of Hodder and Stoughton
Carmelite House
50 Victoria Embankment
London EC4Y 0DZ

An Hachette UK Company

www.hachette.co.uk
www.hachettechildrens.co.uk

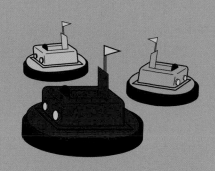

CONTENTS

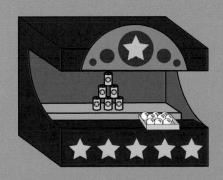

ALL THE FUN OF THE FAIR!

Fairs and festivals have existed for hundreds of years – but when fairs first started, they only had stalls, shows and contests. Big, exciting fairground rides became popular in the 1800s, after steam and electric power had been invented.

Since then, designers have come up with bigger, faster and more exciting fairground rides, like thrilling corkscrew rollercoasters and super-sized big wheels. You can find rides like these at fairs, festivals and parks all over the world.

If you love fairs, theme parks and white-knuckle rides, this book is for you. It shows you how to make a whole fairground of model rides. A lot of them really work too! You'll find out how to design and build your own rollercoaster, make a working big wheel, a whirling flying chair ride, a carousel and lots more.

MAKE IT YOUR OWN!

You can make the projects exactly as instructed, but you don't have to. Feel free to use the instructions as a starting point, then come up with your own designs. You don't have to make every part of the fairground either.

Make a carousel with dragons instead of horses, a terrifyingly tall flying chair ride or a double big wheel. Or go wild and invent your own, completely new fairground ride! After all, today's ride designers do that for a living. One day, that could be your job too!

MAKER MATERIALS

The projects in this book have been designed to work using things you can find at home, such as disposable containers, packaging and basic art and craft equipment. If you don't have what you need, you can usually get it at a hobby or craft store, supermarket or DIY store or by ordering online. See page 31 for a list of useful sources.

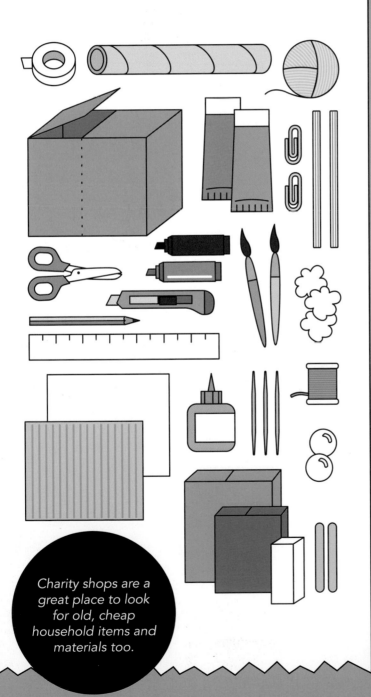

Charity shops are a great place to look for old, cheap household items and materials too.

BLOOP BLOOP! SAFETY ALERT!

For some of the projects, you'll need to use sharp tools such as a craft knife, wire clippers or a bradawl (a pointed tool for making holes). Or you might want to use an electric appliance like a hot glue gun.

For anything involving sharp objects, heat or electricity, always ask an adult to help and supervise. Make sure you keep items like these in a safe place, away from where younger children could find them.

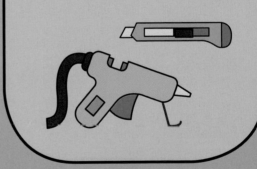

CAN I USE THIS?

Before you start emptying the cupboards, make sure any containers or other household items you want to use are finished with, clean and you have permission to make them into mind-blowing thrill rides. Buckle your seat belt, you're ready to begin!

HeLTeR-SKeLTeR

Dating back over 100 years, a helter-skelter is the ultimate traditional fairground ride.

WHAT YOU NEED

- Two large sheets of smooth white card (size A3 or bigger)
- A paper cup
- Scissors or a craft knife
- Strong sticky tape
- Strong glue or a glue gun
- Paints and paintbrushes or marker pens
- A ruler and a pencil
- A cocktail stick or wooden skewer

For the large sheets of card, you could use the backs of large pads of drawing paper, or card from large packaging boxes, as long as it's smooth and flexible, not corrugated.

1 Curl one sheet of card into a cone shape, with a narrow top about 6 cm across. Sticky tape it together on the inside. Trim the ends so it stands upright.

2 Trim the rim off the paper cup and check that it fits on top of the cone. Trim the top of the cone shape if it doesn't fit.

3 Mark a door and windows onto the paper cup. Carefully cut them out. Glue the cup on top of the cone. Decorate the tower with marker pens or paints and leave to dry.

4 Use a ruler and pencil to mark a row of dots 3 cm apart across the middle of the other sheet of card. Starting in the middle, draw a spiral, passing the line through all the dots. Keep drawing the spiral until you get to the edge of the card.

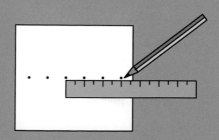
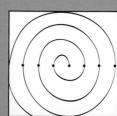

5 Carefully cut the spiral out and decorate it. When the paint is dry, open it out and lower it onto the tower.

6 Adjust the spiral until you can make it wrap around the tower from the top (just below the door) to the bottom, sloping downhill. Cut off any parts you don't need at the ends.

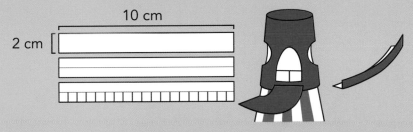

7 Cut small rectangles of card (1 cm wide, 2 cm long) and fold them in half. Glue or tape them along the underneath of the spiral slide and to the sides of the tower, to hold the slide in place.

8 Cut 2-cm-wide and 10-cm-long strips of card. Fold them in half lengthways and cut slits 1 cm apart along one length of each strip to help them curve. Decorate them and glue them along the edge of the slide to make a railing.

9 Cut another door into the base of the tower. Make and decorate a paper flag, glue it to the skewer or cocktail stick and stick it into the top of the tower.

TIP
Traditional helter-skelters often have a red and white striped pattern, but you can use any colour or pattern you like.

THE SCIENCE BIT!
A super-simple fairground ride, the helter-skelter simply uses gravity to pull the rider down to the bottom. The longer you slide, the faster you go!

CHAIR SWING RIDE

The flying chair ride makes riders fly out sideways as they spin around. These rides can be any height – some are close to the ground, and others are high in the sky!

WHAT YOU NEED

- A shallow box, such as a chocolate box with a lid
- Two cardboard tubes, one slightly narrower than the other
- A disc-shaped cardboard box, such as a cheese triangle box
- A pencil
- Scissors or a craft knife
- Strong sticky tape
- Strong glue or a glue gun
- Plain white paper and card
- Paints and paintbrushes or marker pens
- White PVA glue
- Small metal paper clips
- Thin string
- A bradawl or thick needle
- A lolly stick or craft stick

1 Draw around the wider cardboard tube onto the middle of the shallow box lid. Carefully cut out the hole, making it slightly smaller than the line to make a tight fit.

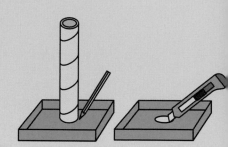

2 Tape the bottom of the tube to the base inside the box. Push the lid back down so that the tube is firmly held in place.

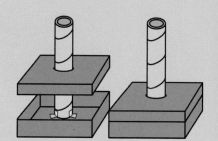

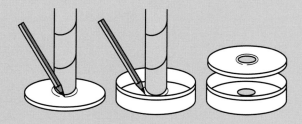

3 Draw around the narrower tube onto the middle of the disc-shaped box's lid. Cut inside the line to make the hole slightly smaller. Do the same on the base of the box.

4 Push the narrower tube through both holes, leaving 2 cm sticking out at the top. Trim the ends of tubes if necessary so that the narrower one fits inside the wider one and the disc can turn.

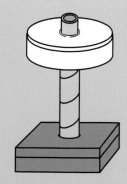

5 Decorate the ride with paint mixed with an equal amount of white PVA glue to make it stick, or cover the ride with white paper and decorate with marker pens.

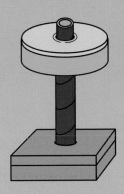

6 Bend a paperclip into a square. Cut a piece of card the same width as the square and four times as long. Cut one end of it into a narrow strip. Fold the card to make a seat that fits over the sides of the square. Glue in place.

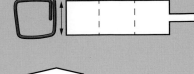
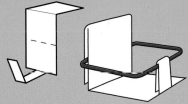
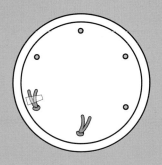

7 Loop a long piece of string under the folded back of the chair. Cut two slots in the front of the chair, and loop another piece of string through them.

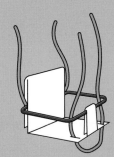

8 Take the lid off the disc-shaped box and make holes around the edge of its base. Feed the ends of the strings through a hole. Adjust them so that the chair hangs straight, then sticky tape in place. Add more chairs all around the disc, then put the lid back on.

9 Using a craft knife or scissors, make a slot through the top of the narrow tube, above the disc. Fit a lolly or craft stick through it, so that you can turn the ride easily.

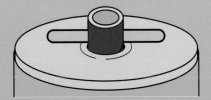

THE SCIENCE BIT!

The flying chair ride works using centrifugal force. As an object is whirled around in a circle, centrifugal force also makes it pull outwards. This makes the chairs fly out sideways.

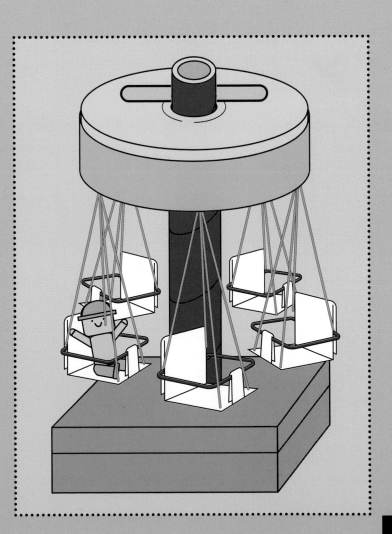

FAIRGROUND STALLS

Any good funfair has plenty of stalls, where you can try out your skills and win a prize.

WHAT YOU NEED

- Small and medium-sized square cardboard boxes
- Medium-sized round (cardboard) box
- A round plastic lid at least 2 cm deep
- Plain white paper and card
- Scissors or a craft knife
- Strong glue or a glue gun
- Sticky tape
- Paints and paintbrushes or marker pens
- White PVA glue
- A bradawl or thick needle
- A pencil
- A paper bowl
- Four non-bendy straws
- Metal paper clips
- A sheet of craft foam
- A silver pen
- Small round beads

FOR TIN CAN ALLEY STAND:

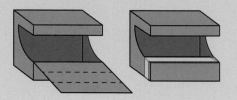

1 Mark a stall shape onto a cube-shaped cardboard box. Cut out the sides. At the front, fold the cardboard over inside the box twice, to make a counter. Tape it down.

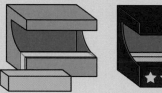

2 Use a smaller box, such as a toothpaste box, to make another counter at the back of the stall. Decorate the stall with marker pens or paints mixed with PVA glue to make it stick. Leave to dry.

3 Cut a sign shape out of card, decorate it and glue or tape it to the front of the stall. For the cans, roll paper strips into cylinders. Colour them silver and decorate them if you like. Stack them in pyramids on the back counter.

4 Cut the end off a small box to make a tray, and colour it silver too. Glue it to the front counter and fill with beads to use as balls for knocking down the cans.

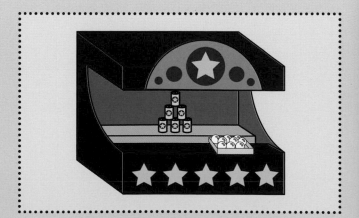

FOR A HOOK-A-DUCK STALL:

1 Draw around the round plastic lid onto the middle of the round box. Cut out the circle just inside the line. Glue the lid into the hole to make a shallow pool.

2 Use a bradawl or thick needle to make four holes around the sides of the box. Enlarge the holes with a pencil. Fit four straws into the holes and tape or glue in place inside the round box.

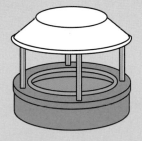

3 Trim the straws down to about 10 cm. Glue an upturned paper bowl on top as a roof. Add a cardboard sign too if you like. Decorate the stall and leave to dry.

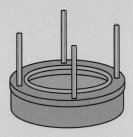

4 Make ducks from craft foam by cutting out small ovals and neck and head shapes with downward-pointing beaks. Make slots in the ovals and fit the necks into them.

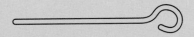

5 To make the hooks, straighten out metal paper clips and bend one end into a hook shape. Carefully pour water into the pool and float the ducks on it.

TAKE IT FURTHER ...
• To add prizes, make hooks from paper clips and attach them to the stalls. Hang up tiny dolls, balls or other toys.
• Can you design and make other types of stalls, such as a hoopla or a coconut shy?

TIP
You can have a go on these stalls yourself, even though they're model-sized! Try hooking a duck by its beak with the tiny hook, or put a bead on the front counter and flick it at the tin cans.

BIG WHEEL

A big wheel, or Ferris wheel, is one of the most spectacular sights at the fairground. They are also popular attractions outside fairgrounds, with increasingly bigger wheels being built in city centres around the world.

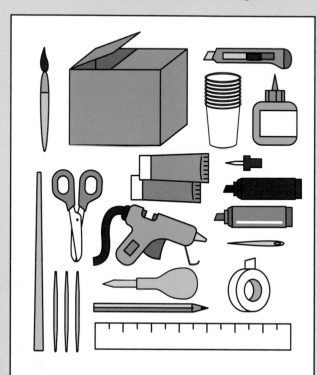

WHAT YOU NEED

- A large, strong corrugated cardboard box (at least 35 cm tall)
- A chopstick
- Cocktail sticks or wooden skewers
- A bradawl or thick needle
- 8 paper cups
- A pinboard pin
- Scissors or a craft knife
- Strong glue or a glue gun
- Strong sticky tape
- A ruler and a pencil
- Paints and paintbrushes or marker pens

1 On one side of the box, mark a line about 4 cm up from the base. Draw a large triangle in the middle about 30 cm tall and 20 cm wide at the base.

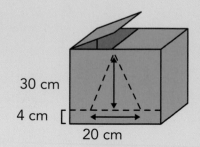

2 Cut out the triangle and 4-cm strip and half of the base of the box too, so that you have a piece that looks like this.

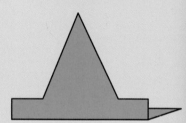

3 Do the same with the other side of the box, making two matching pieces. Trim each base piece to about 5 cm wide. Fix them together using strong sticky tape.

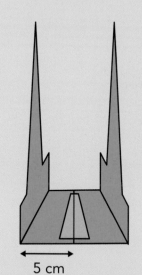

4 Cut two 3-cm-wide circles of cardboard. Glue them inside each of the triangle-shaped sides at the top. Use a bradawl or thick needle to make holes through the middle of the circle and tip of the triangle.

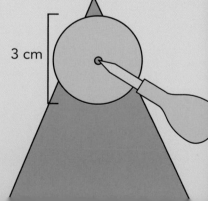

5 Use a pencil to make the holes bigger. Push the chopstick through the holes. Check it can turn easily. You can now decorate the base with paint or marker pens.

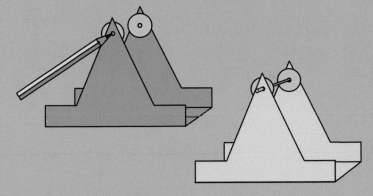

6 Take the two sides of the box that you haven't used yet. Mark a circle on each of them, each about 30 cm wide. (Draw around an object that's roughly the right size, like a large dinner plate.)

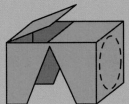

7 Cut the circles out. Mark a dot in the middle of each circle and use a ruler to draw a line across it. Draw another line at right angles, and two more lines between them to make eight spokes.

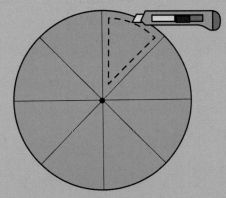

8 In one of the sections, draw a triangle 1 cm inside the edges. Carefully cut it out, then use it as a template to draw and cut out triangles in the rest of the sections. Do this for both wheels.

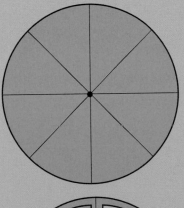
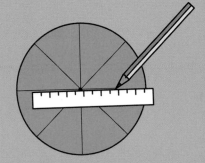
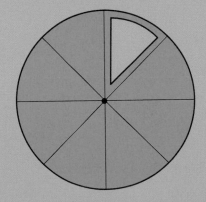

TURN THE PAGE TO CONTINUE ...

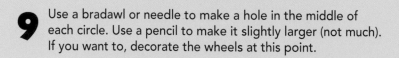

9 Use a bradawl or needle to make a hole in the middle of each circle. Use a pencil to make it slightly larger (not much). If you want to, decorate the wheels at this point.

10 Put the two wheels inside the base piece. Thread the chopstick through the holes in the base and through the two wheels. It should fit tightly on the wheels. Move the wheels apart so that they almost touch the sides of the base.

11 Check that you can turn the chopstick handle around to make the wheels turn. Line up the spokes in the two wheels. At the end of each spoke, make small holes through both wheels with the bradawl or needle.

12 Now make the eight baskets. For each basket, mark a basket shape on a paper cup, with two arms pointing upwards at the sides. Cut out the basket shapes.

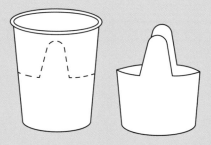

13 Make holes through the tops of the arms, and make them larger using a pencil (or you could use a hole punch to make them). If you want to, decorate the baskets now.

14 Push a wooden skewer or cocktail stick through a hole in one wheel, through the basket arm holes and through the other wheel. Trim off the ends if they stick out.

15 Repeat step 14 for all the baskets, until the wheel is complete. Once all the baskets are in place, check that they are able to swing freely when you turn the wheel (if not, move the arm holes down).

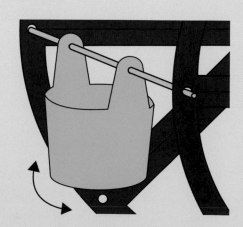

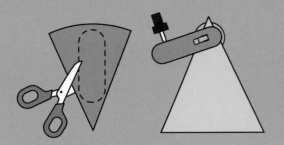

16 Cut a 2-cm-wide and 5-cm-long strip of cardboard. Cut a small square hole in one end. Fit it onto the chopstick handle. Stick a pinboard pin in the other end to make a turning handle.

TIP
You may need to adjust the position of the wheel, chopstick or base slightly to make everything work smoothly.

TIP
Sit small toy figures in the baskets to ride the big wheel!

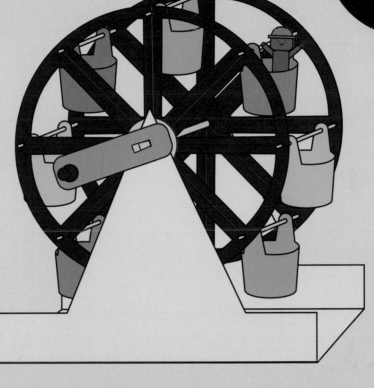

THE SCIENCE BIT!

The world's biggest Ferris wheels are over 160 m tall! That's as high as a skyscraper with 50 floors. Instead of open baskets, these super-giant wheels often have enclosed pods or capsules. Some have as many as 60 of them!

TAKE IT FURTHER ...

Real big wheels often have lights, making them look even more amazing when night falls. You could light up your big wheel by attaching activated glow sticks, or using small battery-operated fairy lights (making sure they don't get tangled as the wheel turns).

DODGEMS

Dodgems or bumper cars zoom around on a flat rink, crashing into each other. They're easy to make from a few bits of packaging.

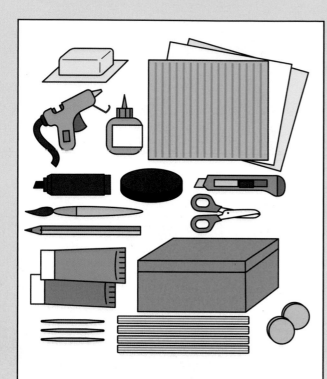

WHAT YOU NEED

- Wide round plastic lids from food containers – black if possible
- Plastic blister packs from small items such as batteries, erasers or dental floss
- Thick corrugated card
- Smooth plain card
- Cocktail sticks
- Small buttons or flat beads
- Scissors or a craft knife
- Strong glue or a glue gun
- Paint and paintbrushes
- White PVA glue
- A pencil and a marker pen
- A large cardboard box with a lid, such as a shoe box
- Four non-bendy straws
- Coloured or metallic card (optional)

1 Turn your lid flat side facing up. If it's not black, paint it black using paint mixed with white PVA glue to help it stick. Leave to dry.

2 Draw and cut out a circle of thick corrugated card, just slightly smaller than your lid. Cut out the plastic blister pack shape, leaving a small area of flat plastic around the edges.

3 Glue the flat part of the blister pack to the circle of card. Draw an H shape on top of the blister pack and cut along the lines. Fold down the flaps inside the blister pack.

4 Cut out a strip of card, the same width as the hole you've made in the blister pack and four times as long. Fold it to make a seat and seat back. Glue it into the hole.

5 Paint the seat and upper part of the bumper car all over with paint mixed with white PVA glue, and leave to dry. Then glue them to the black lid 'bumper'.

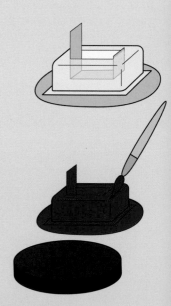

6 Cut a small steering wheel out of card, colour it black and glue into the front of the seat. Add 'headlights' made from beads or buttons and a paper flag attached to a cocktail stick. Repeat steps 1 to 6 to make more bumper cars.

7 To make a rink, cut the bottom 3 cm off the base of your large box. Tape four straws into the corners, standing upright.

8 Fit the box lid onto the tops of the straws. Tape in place. Cut out a cardboard sign and tape or glue to the front. Paint or decorate the rink. Cover the floor with brightly coloured or metallic card.

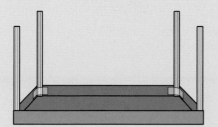

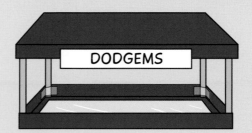

DODGEMS

DODGEMS

THE SCIENCE BIT!

On real-life bumper cars, the black bumper is made of rubber. When it gets hit, it squashes, absorbing the shock, so the car itself doesn't get damaged. Normal cars have shock-absorbing bumpers as well.

TAKE IT FURTHER ...

To help your cars move around, try putting a handful of marbles under the lid part of each one.

CAROUSEL

The carousel is a famous, old-fashioned horse ride. Riders sit on brightly painted horses, which leap up and down as they whirl around to the sound of fairground music.

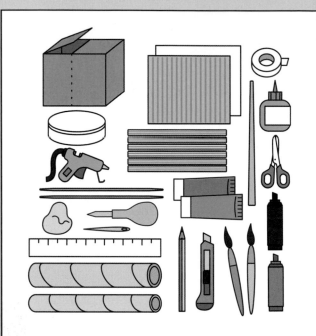

WHAT YOU NEED

- A round cardboard box lid, such as the lid from a round chocolate box
- Two cardboard tubes, one slightly narrower than the other
- Thick, strong corrugated card, such as the side of a large cardboard box
- 12 wooden skewers
- Six non-bendy straws
- A wooden chopstick or similar wooden stick
- Smooth plain white card
- Scissors or a craft knife
- A bradawl or thick needle
- A ruler and a pencil
- Paints and paintbrushes or marker pens
- White PVA glue
- Strong glue or a glue gun
- Strong sticky tape
- Sticky tack or soft modelling clay

1 Cut about eight slots around the top of the wider cardboard tube, about 1 cm deep. Fold the tabs inward, and glue them to the inside of the round lid, right in the middle.

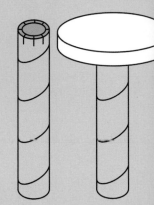

2 Turn the lid over and draw around it onto thick corrugated card. Cut this circle out to make the base of the carousel. Then stand the bottom of the wider tube in the middle of the circle and draw around it.

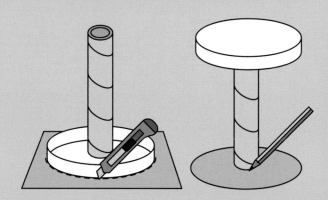

TROUBLESHOOTING!

This four-page project includes the option to make the horses move up and down, like they do on a real carousel. However, this is quite tricky, so you also have the option of just making them move round and round, by only working up to step 13.

3 Cut the small circle out of the middle of the base and fit the tube into the hole. Use glue or tape to fix it together if necessary. At this point, you can decorate the carousel with marker pens or paints mixed with white PVA glue. Leave to dry.

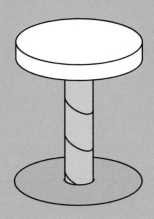

4 Mark six equally spaced points around the base, just in from the edge. Make holes through them with the bradawl or needle. Cut six pieces of straw, about 8 cm long.

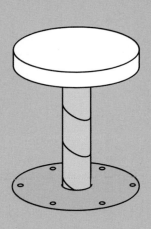

5 Push a wooden skewer up through one of the holes in the base, then through a section of straw. Then push the top of the skewer up inside the lid, so that it lies flat against the inside edge of the lid.

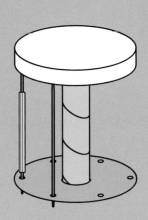

6 Use strong tape to fix the end of the skewer inside the lid, making sure it stands straight upright between the base and the lid. Repeat this for the other five skewers and straws.

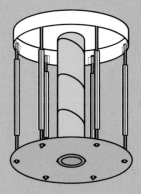

7 With scissors, cut off the bottom of each skewer as neatly as possible, so that the base is flat and smooth underneath. Use a little glue or tape to fix the skewers in place if necessary.

8 Measure the distance between the skewers. Copy a picture of a carousel horse onto smooth white card, making it slightly shorter than the distance you measured.

9 Cut out the horse and use it as a template to draw 11 more. Decorate them and cut them out. Glue two horses to each straw, one on either side, about $2/3$ of the way up.

TURN THE PAGE TO CONTINUE ...

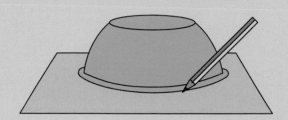

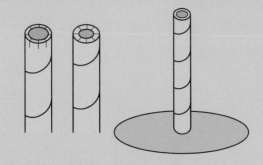

10 Draw around a plate or other object onto thick corrugated card to make a circle larger than the carousel. For example, if your carousel is 20 cm wide, make the larger circle about 25 cm wide. Cut it out.

11 Take the narrower cardboard tube, and cut slots into one end of it, as you did with the wider one. Fold the slots inward, and glue the tube to the middle of the large circle.

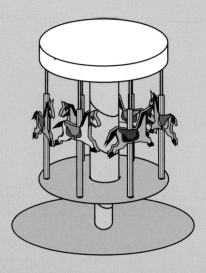

12 If necessary, trim off the top of the narrower tube, to make it shorter than your carousel. You can now fit your carousel onto it, so that it rests on the larger circle and can turn around.

13 Make a hole in the middle of the top of your carousel, and push the chopstick or other stick down into it. You can use this to turn the carousel around.

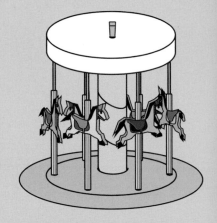

TAKE IT FURTHER ...
Want to make the horses jump up and down too? Follow steps 14–19!

14 Cut a long strip of smooth card, about 6 cm wide and four times longer than the width of your carousel. Draw a 1-cm-wide line along its length.

15 Wrap the card strip around the carousel to make a circle about 2 cm wider than the base. Glue or tape it together and trim off any extra.

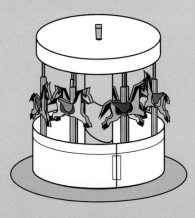

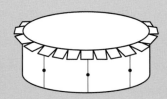

16 Slip the circle off the carousel. Cut slots along its edge, up to the line you drew. Fold the slots outwards. Mark six equal points around the circle. Draw lines to divide it into six sections.

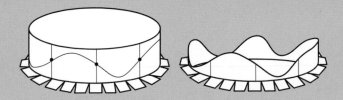

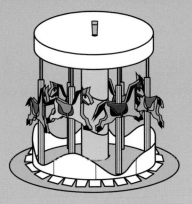

17 Draw a wavy line around the circle, going up and down with each section. Cut along the wavy line. Now glue it to the base around the carousel, leaving a bit of space all the way round.

18 Cut six very small strips of smooth card. Glue them to the bottom ends of the straws to make loops. Each one should face the same way as the horse's head.

19 Take a new skewer and thread it through a loop. Put a pea-sized lump of sticky tack or modelling clay on the end. Press it against the bottom of the central tube. Repeat for the other five horses. Trim off the ends, so that the skewers rest on the wavy cardboard circle.

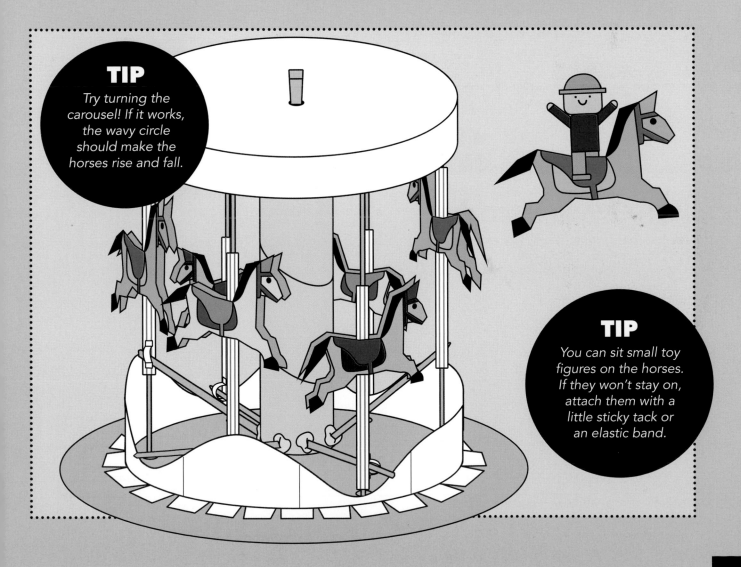

TIP

Try turning the carousel! If it works, the wavy circle should make the horses rise and fall.

TIP

You can sit small toy figures on the horses. If they won't stay on, attach them with a little sticky tack or an elastic band.

ROLLERCOASTER

Are you ready for the most frightening fairground attraction of all, the rollercoaster? Some people love rollercoasters and travel the world trying out all the most terrifying rides. Others won't go near them. But since you don't have to ride this coaster yourself, you can make it as hair-raising as you like.

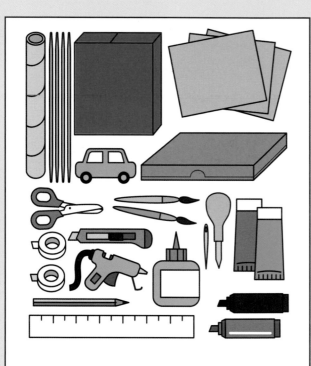

WHAT YOU NEED

- A large, strong, shallow cardboard box, such as a pizza box
- Smaller cardboard boxes
- Plenty of thick, smooth card
- Several long cardboard tubes, such as wrapping paper tubes
- Wooden skewers
- A small toy car
- Scissors or a craft knife
- Strong glue or a glue gun
- Strong sticky tape
- Masking tape
- A bradawl or thick needle
- A ruler and a pencil
- Paints and paintbrushes
- Felt-tip or marker pens

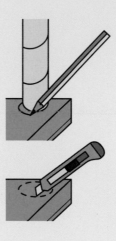

1 Draw around a cardboard tube onto the corner of your large, shallow box. Carefully cut out the circle, slightly inside the line, so that the tube will fit tightly. Fit the tube into the hole.

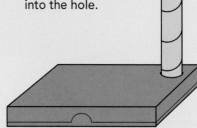

2 Do the same in the other corners of the box. This will give you enough towers to get started. You can add more later if you need to.

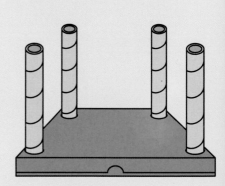

3 Before making the track, sketch a design for your rollercoaster on paper. The track should join up in a loop, with a very high starting point so that the car rolls downhill.

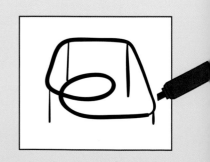

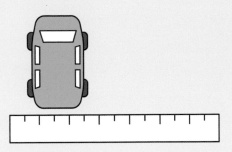

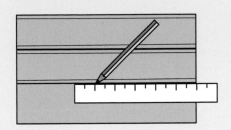

4 To make the track, first check the width of your toy car. The track should be around 2 cm wider than the car, so that it fits easily around the bends.

5 With a ruler and pencil, draw lengths of track onto smooth card, making them the right width. Add an extra 2 cm strip along each side of the track, to make the sides.

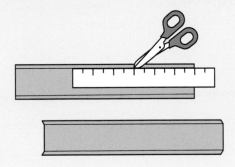

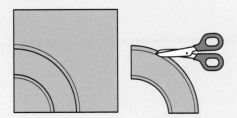

6 Cut out the pieces of track. Use a ruler and a scissor blade to press, or score, along the lines so that the sides can fold up easily.

7 Make corners by drawing curved sections of track. Use a ruler to make sure you keep the track the same width all the way along and add sides. Cut out and score these pieces too.

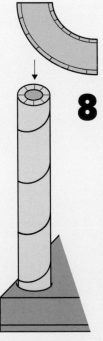

8 Now you can start building the coaster. Start at the top of the tallest tube. Cut 1 cm slots into the top of the tube, fold them inwards and glue a piece of track on top. You can use sticky tape to strengthen the join too.

9 To make a section of track bend up or down, cut slots along the sides. Also cut slots along the sides of the curved pieces.

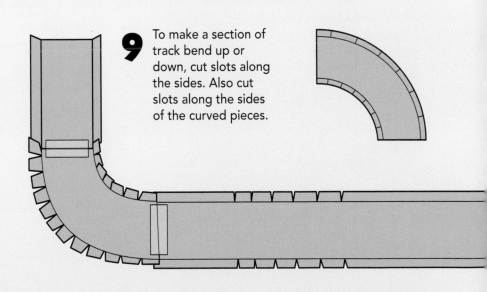

TURN THE PAGE TO CONTINUE ...

10 Add more sections as you go, taping them together with strong sticky tape. You can cut each piece of track to the length you need or draw new sections to fit your design.

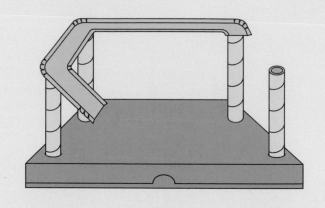

11 Cut each tube to the right height to support your track and fix the track onto it. If you need to, add more tubes to the box or use wooden skewers as extra supports.

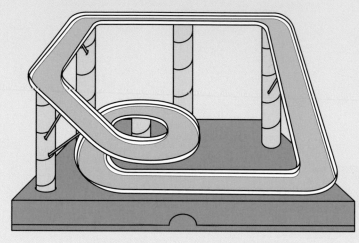

12 When your track is finished, fold the sides up all along the edges. Fold lengths of masking tape (or just normal sticky tape) over the sides to hold them in place. You can now decorate your coaster with paint or marker pens.

13 To make your coaster car, cut a piece off a small cardboard box, such as a toothpaste tube box, to make a long tray shape. Make sure it is as narrow as the car. Put it on top of your toy car. Use sticky tape to hold it on making sure the wheels can still turn.

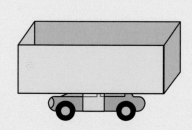

14 Use smaller pieces of cardboard to divide the car into sections, with sticking-up seat backs. If you want to, decorate the coaster car with paints or marker pens.

15 Test the car on your coaster to see if it runs down the track. Fix any sticking points by smoothing them down with sticky tape, or adjusting the track.

16 If there's space on your coaster, you can use another cardboard box to make a ticket office, with a doorway leading to the track and a sign on top.

TICKETS

TIP

It can be tricky to make a rollercoaster track that the car will run all the way down. It needs to be smooth, with steep enough slopes for the car to build up speed, without going so fast that it flies off at the corners! Try making a fairly simple coaster for your first attempt, to practise your skills. Then you can move on to more adventurous designs.

TAKE IT FURTHER ...

Once you're a master coaster builder, you could try adding more features, like these:

- Can you build in a loop-the-loop?
- Could you build in a gap in the track that the car jumps across?
- Can you add more coaster cars and link them to make a train?

THE SCIENCE BIT!

This rollercoaster relies on gravity to make it work. If your car builds enough speed on a downhill section, it will have enough momentum to go up a small slope. But overall, the track must head downhill.

TICKETS

THE FAIRGROUND

Now make a fabulous fairground for all your rides and stalls!

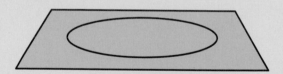

1 Trim your cardboard base to make it the shape you want. It can be any shape, as long as it's big enough to fit all the fairground equipment you have made inside.

2 Most fairgrounds are grassy, so paint the base green all over. Alternatively, you could cover it with green cloth to make it look like grass.

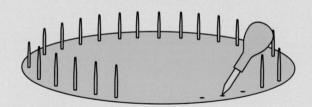

3 For the fence, make a row of holes along the edge of the card using the bradawl or needle. Stick a cocktail stick into each hole. Or you can use pieces cut from straws. Make the holes bigger using the pencil and fit a piece of straw into each hole. Remember to leave a gap in the fence for the entrance.

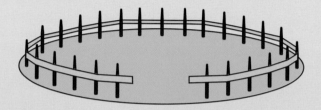

4 Cut long 1-cm-wide strips of card. Glue them along the row of cocktail sticks or straws, just below the top. If you like, carefully paint the fence.

WHAT YOU NEED

- A very large piece of cardboard, or several smaller pieces
- Thick smooth card
- A cereal box
- Straws or cocktail sticks
- Scissors or a craft knife
- Strong glue or a glue gun
- Strong sticky tape
- A bradawl or thick needle
- A pencil
- Paint and paintbrushes
- White PVA glue
- Marker pens
- Lots of green fabric (optional)

You can get a really big piece of cardboard from the box of a large appliance, such as a washing machine. If you can't find one, tape several smaller pieces of cardboard together.

5 To make a grand gateway, draw an archway on the front of the cereal box. Cut out the doorway from both the front and the back of the box.

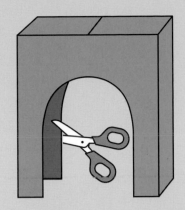

7 Cut out a sign shape, and glue or tape it to the top of the gateway. Decorate the gateway and sign with paint mixed with white PVA glue. When it's dry, fit it into the space in the fence. (Remove part of the fence if necessary.) Arrange your rides and stalls inside.

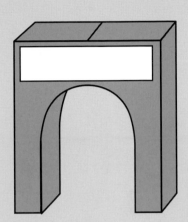

6 Cut a long strip of card (the length of the outline of the archway) to fit in the gap between the front and back of the archway with an extra 1 cm along each side. Cut slots into the edge to make tabs. Carefully glue this strip along the inside edge of the doorway.

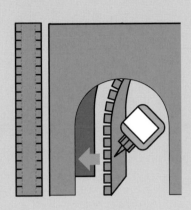

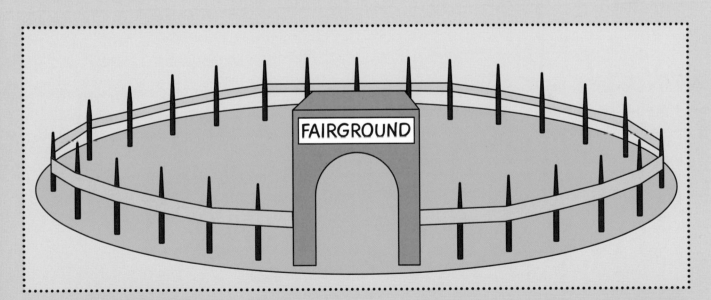

FAIRGROUND

TAKE IT FURTHER ...
Some fairs move from place to place, and the people who work there sleep in caravans on the site. Can you make some workers' caravans?

AND HERE IS YOUR FINISHED FAIRGROUND!

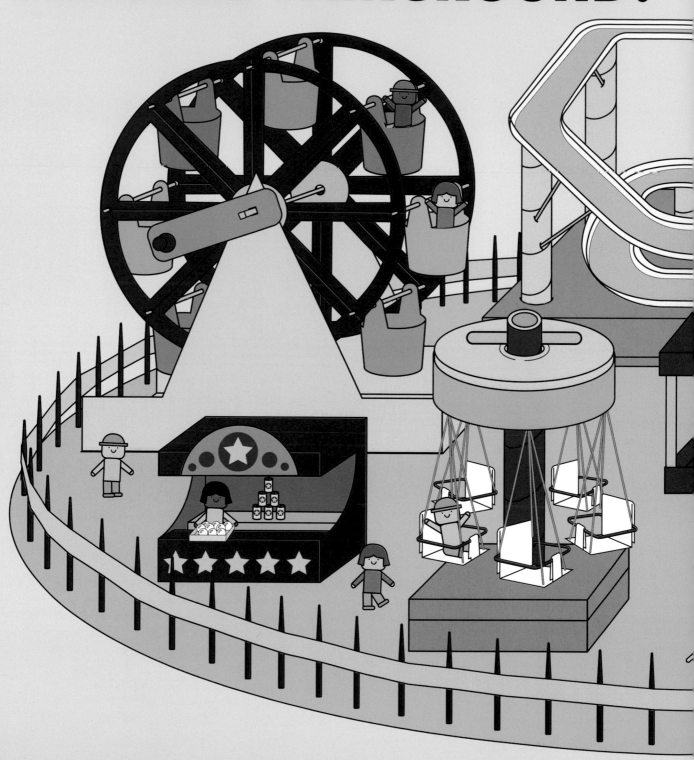

TICKETS

DODGEMS

FAIRGROUND

GLOSSARY

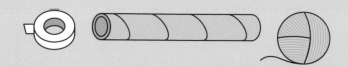

Blister pack Packaging made of a plastic bubble or blister that fits closely around the product.

Bradawl A sharp, pointed tool for making neat holes.

Carousel A fairground ride that spins around in a circle, usually with animals or vehicles to sit on or in.

Centrifugal force A pulling effect that makes objects move outwards when they are whirled around in a circle.

Coconut shy A game at a fair where you throw balls at a row of coconuts and try to knock them down to win them.

Corkscrew rollercoaster
A rollercoaster with a section of track that twists around itself like a corkscrew.

Corrugated cardboard Thick cardboard with a layer of folded rows of paper inside it to make it stronger, often used to make cardboard boxes.

Glue gun A gun-shaped electric tool that heats up and applies strong glue.

Gravity Pulling force on objects. Earth's gravity pulls people and objects down to the ground.

Hoopla Fairground stall game in which players try to throw hoops over prizes.

Ferris wheel A giant rotating wheel with seats or cabins around the edge, named after its inventor George Ferris.

Helter-skelter A slide that travels in a downward spiral around the outside of a tower.

Momentum A force that makes a moving object keep on moving.

Shock absorber A material or object that squashes when something hits it, absorbing the impact.

Spoke Each of the rods that join the edge of a wheel to its centre, giving the wheel its strength.

Template Something that is used as a basic shape or pattern to make lots of copies of.

FURTHER INFORMATION

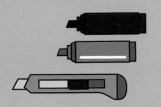

WHERE TO GET MATERIALS

Everyday items
You'll probably have some everyday items and craft materials at home already, such as foil, pens, tissues, string, paper and card, sticky tape, glue and scissors.

Recycling
Old packaging that's going to be thrown away or recycled is a great source of making materials, such as cardboard boxes, yoghurt pots, blister packs, cardboard tubes, magazines, old wrapping paper and newspaper.

Supermarkets
Great for basic items you might not have at home, such as paper cups, cotton wool, a sewing kit, paper straws, wooden skewers and battery-powered fairy lights.

Outdoors
Collect things like leaves, twigs, acorns and seashells for free!

Specialist shops
Hobby and craft shops, sewing shops, art shops, garden centres and DIY stores could be useful for things like a craft knife, a glue gun, PVA glue, modelling clay, fabric, sand and pebbles. If you don't have the shop you need near you, ask an adult to help you look for online shops, such as Hobbycraft.

Charity shops
It's always a good idea to check charity shops when you can, as they often have all kinds of handy household items and craft materials at very low prices.

BOOKS

Fairground Rides (Awesome Engineering) by Sally Spray, Franklin Watts, 2017

How to Design the World's Best Roller Coaster: In 10 Simple Steps by Paul Mason, Wayland, 2016

Junk Modelling by Annalees Lim, Wayland, 2016

Roller Coasters (Calling All Innovators: A Career for You?) by Kevin Cunningham, Scholastic, 2013

Scientriffic: Roller Coaster Science by Chris Oxlade, Red Lemon Press, 2014

WEBSITES

Amusement Park Physics
https://www.learner.org/interactives/parkphysics/
Interactive games and science facts about fairground rides

PBS Design Squad
https://pbskids.org/designsquad/
Lots of brilliant design and build challenges

DIY
https://diy.org/
An online maker community for kids

Parents.com Arts & Crafts
https://www.parents.com/fun/arts-crafts/?page=1
Maker projects, instructions and videos

Kiwico DIY page
https://www.kiwico.com/diy/
Fun and easy maker ideas

INDEX

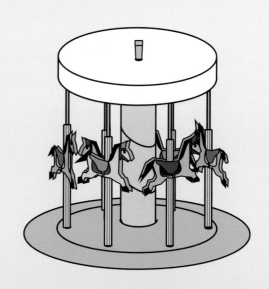